Practical Inspired Quotes

Monica L. Sanders, M.Div

Dedicated to those who have inspired me, talked about me, hurt me and used me. Each experience gave a practical meaning to my life and caused me to be stronger and to continue to live a life of excellence no matter the criticism from others.

I thank God for HIS
peace to still
love and care.

"For God so loved the
world he gave HIS
only begotten Son."
-John 3:16

Practically Inspired quotes were laid upon my heart as I moved through this journey called life. I have shared these with others and hope that they inspire you to be your best and not to let anyone make you sin in thought, word or deed (knowingly and unknowingly).
They may not heal your life but they will help your life.

- Show Up
- Glow Up
- Blow Up

Grown people
take
responsibility
and do
not hide their
transgressions.

Consistently thinking about it doesn't get it done.

Disappointment
is hurtful and
must be
forgiven.

It's hard to be silent when you are screaming inside.

Be sure, be safe and be responsible.

Stop thinking everybody is happy for you.

Pray until the storm passes.

Become a Titus 2 Woman!

Resentment is the foundation of disappointment and anger.

Your prayers
are someone's
stone mover,
ask Lazarus.

You got to love
or leave it.

Be that
instrument of
peace and love.

Let your faith remove your doubt.

Keep moving
quietly,
folks cannot
attack what
they don't hear.

Don't be alarmed, be intentional.

Be a meteorite, not a <u>meteor</u>. There is a difference.

Do for others,
as God does for
you.

All will be judged, no worries.

Make resolutions, not rituals.

Give God your
first and
watch how you
become HIS
priority.

Prayer, Power & Authority: Makes one extraordinary force.

A strong,
committed
woman of
GOD,
cannot be
destroyed.

A Woman of God can be recognized, even by a blind man.
It's her spirit and anointing, not the way she looks.

Build God's vision for you, NOT your dream for yourself.

Increase in
God's capacity
so, HE can
decrease your
concerns.

Don't let your situation/ circumstance dictate to you. God is still in control.

Disconnection
means no
power, no
strength.
Stay connected
to Godly
sources.

Patiently
waiting until
The Lord give
instruction.

They tried, the
enemy tried,
however I am
still here.

Broken,
Wounded and
now its time to
ask for help.

Remember
those who
prayed for you,
because you
would not be
where you are if
they didn't.

Make the right
relationship
contacts.
Don't waste
your time on
folks,
who want to
waste your
time.

Refuse to panic, especially, if you already prayed.

Repent, Pray, & Prepare.

You cannot
expect a harvest
IF, you didn't
plant anything.

Don't be an enabler, hold people accountable.

Appearance is important, Presence is inviting however, your intellect is mind-blowing.

Represent well,
at all times.

Walk in
excellence
and
watch where it
takes you.

To get in formation, you must have the right information.

Be a catalyst in
a chaotic world.

Time is a gift,
how will you
share it today.

Stay in your lane, before you get run over.

When you wear
the spirit of
offense,
you will be
offended.

Be a voice and
not an echo, we
have too many
of those.
Hello! Hello!
Hello!

A loss should consist of a refocus.

Stop giving what you don't have.

If you are going to be frustrated, don't tolerate it.

God's hand IS
unchanging,
hold on tight
and don't ever
let go.

How can you
refill others if
you are empty.

Always Be
Godly and Do
Godly things.

Be careful what
you say,
You may have
to eat those
words for
dinner.

Be mindful of
how you treat
God's people,
He is watching
and may not be
so forgiving.

There are some things that you just know, don't apologize or fill condemned for it.

Perception is dangerous especially, when others are perceiving.

Communication is key, however you must make access.

Be quick to
forgive and
move on.
Time is too
precious.

Find yourself
and revisit your
goals.

Pray More.

Re-launch, you still have time.

Don't be a worrier, find your warrior.

Be Proactive, Not Reactive.

Be Consistent
Be Committed
Be Present

Don't bargain
with your
peace.

Be brutally
honest with
yourself,
so you can be
honest with
others.

Listen, when truth is being spoken.

Overcome Bitterness, they still don't care.

Don't be
convicted or
condemned
unless
God is your
judge.

Just DO, Christ!

My last quote is from my
mother,
(Reverend Claretha Basil)
Growing up, she would
say,
"My mind don't lead me
wrong."
As kids we would look at
each other and say, what!?

It was her way of saying
she knew something but
didn't say anything about
it however it was true.

Please don't take yourself too seriously, enjoy life. I hope you can take time and add your inspiration to this book. Remember to believe in yourself because if you don't no one else will.

My Inspirational Quote

_____

_____

_____

_____

_____

_____

_____

Other books by Monica L. Sanders

A Heart Matter
Beyond The Veil
Pocketbook of Prayers
21 Day(s) Consecration
Journal

www.ingramcontent.com/pod-product-compliance
Lightning Source LLC
Chambersburg PA
CBHW032211040426
42449CB00005B/542